Thank You Grandma
for Teaching me to Pray

Barbara A. Jones

WestBow Press books may be ordered through booksellers or by contacting:

WestBow Press
A Division of Thomas Nelson & Zondervan
1663 Liberty Drive
Bloomington, IN 47403
www.westbowpress.com
844-714-3454

Interior Image Credit: Chad Thompson

Scripture quotations marked (MSG) are taken from The Message, copyright © 1993, 2002, 2018 by Eugene H. Peterson. Used by permission of NavPress. All rights reserved. Represented by Tyndale House Publishers.

Scripture quotations marked NIV are taken from the Holy Bible, New International Version®, NIV®. Copyright © 1973, 1978, 1984 by Biblica, Inc.™ Used by permission of Zondervan. All rights reserved worldwide.

Scripture quotations marked NLT are taken from the Holy Bible, New Living Translation, copyright © 1996, 2004, 2007 by Tyndale House Foundation. Used by permission of Tyndale House Publishers, Inc., Carol Stream, Illinois 60188. All rights reserved.

ISBN: 979-8-3850-2394-3 (sc)
ISBN: 979-8-3850-2396-7 (hc)
ISBN: 979-8-3850-2395-0 (e)

Library of Congress Control Number: 2024908077

Print information available on the last page.

WestBow Press rev. date: 10/29/2024

WESTBOW
PRESS®
A DIVISION OF THOMAS NELSON
& ZONDERVAN

Thank You Grandma
for Teaching me to Pray

During the COVID pandemic in 2020, Kim did not have a formal graduation but was still class salutatorian! Schools closed, classes converted to online, and several graduations were canceled. Kim's family received approval to have an honoring ceremony at home, which was awesome.

After a few weeks of just chilling, Kim wanted more, she wanted to work to help with college. She saw an ad at *Burley Bread* bakery-sandwich counter, scanned the QR code, applied for a job, said a prayer and boom got a call, interview, and was hired. Her prayers were answered. John 16:24 MSG *"Ask in my name, according to my will, and he'll most certainly give it to you. Your joy will be a river overflowing its banks!"* The money would help with what she needed for college. Kim really enjoyed working as a Restaurant Team Member/Cashier but wanted to be a Forensic Science Technician which required 4-years of college and strong science skills. Kim would be the first in the family to attend college and was really excited about it!

2

Summer was coming and soon Kim's job would be ending. She applied to several colleges and only received a response from one, and it was a thank you for your interest, you have been waitlisted. She did not know why there were no other responses, the applications were complete, financial aid forms complete, obtained recommendation letters, surely being class salutatorian with a 3.8 GPA, the letter from the Pastor and Guidance Counselor meant something.

Kim asked her grandma, "why was it taking so long to get a response to her college applications?" Her grandma said, "sometimes God is not responding because He's working on other things before, he can respond." Kim asked her what that meant. She said, "you know when you are preparing chicken for dinner, you must wait until the oil is hot, to fry the chicken. If you rush, the chicken will not fry thoroughly, may take longer to cook, or burn on the outside. Once the oil is hot, then you can place the chicken in the oil, not touching each other, and turn when brown. Meanwhile the cabbage and rice are already prepared but cannot be served until the chicken is cooked!" Kim asked grandma, what cooking chicken had to do with college applications? She said, "girl it's a metaphor, I wanted to make it understandable for you. The word says, pray about all things. Philippians 4:6-7 MSG *"Don't fret or worry. Instead of worrying, pray. Let petitions and praises shape your worries into prayers, letting God know your concerns. Before you know it, a sense of God's wholeness, everything coming together for good, will come and settle you down. It's wonderful what happens when Christ displaces worry at the center of your life."* So, you are saying when I get ready to fry chicken, make sure the oil is hot, and do not forget to tell God what I need and be thankful! I am just joking with you Grandma I got it."

When Kim went to bed that night, she prayed and asked God to give her understanding and patience as she waits for a response to her college applications. She woke the next morning and realized she had one of the most restful nights sleeps that she has had in a while thinking to herself, "surely if God healed Ms. Rose during COVID, He would give me patience now." Psalm 37:7 MSG *"Quiet down before GOD, BE prayerful before him. Don't bother with those who climb the ladder, who elbow their way to the top."*

As Kim prepared for work, she could hear her grandma praying, "and give baby-girl patience and understanding that it is in the waiting that she grows. God may your will be done." Kim really loved hearing her grandma praying, it was something about her prayer that made everything feel better. Even though her Grandma prayed for patience, it was still on her mind. When her mom took her to work, she asked what was wrong. She told her that not getting a response from the college applications was in her thoughts. It was April and she had not heard anything. Her mom told her to have faith and trust in the Lord, He knows what He's doing. "Yeah, yeah that's what Grandma says, I sure wish I knew what He was doing!" Psalm 62:7-8 NIV *"My salvation and my honor depend on God[a]; he is my mighty rock, my refuge. 8 Trust in him at all times, you people; pour out your hearts to him, for God is our refuge."*

After Kim got to work, one of the regular customers asked her what college she was going to and she replied, "I don't know, haven't heard anything from my apps." The customer said, "don't worry, I'm sure you'll hear something soon."

When Kim's mother picked her up from work, she asked if there was any mail. Her mother said, "I'm not sure, we'll see when we get home." As soon as Kim arrived home, she asked about mail, her grandma said, "something came for you I put it on the table." Her little brother was at the table playing his PlayStation 5 and refused to move so she could see what was under the game. "Quit playing," she screamed, "I'm looking for mail about college."

As she tried to move his game from atop the mail she said, "grandma make him stop!" Grandma said, "give her the mail and stop being so extra." Kim's brother sighed and gave her the mail. "Oh man they're here, they're here my college application responses!" She begins to flex and fan the five envelopes, Mom, Grandma how do I open these? They both replied laughing, "one at a time" grandma said "before we open let us have a word of prayer, Dear Lord we don't know what the letters say but we ask that you grant us good responses so that my granddaughter may move forward in the next chapter of her life. Amen."

As Kim began to open the letters, three of the letters were acceptance letters. Check this out, they were for the schools that she wanted to attend, University of MD Eastern Shore, Morgan University, and Frostburg, all Criminal Justice program. Kim said, "It looks like the grease got hot, so the chicken is cooking!" When you pray about situations and trust God, He works it out. Proverbs 3:5-6 MSG *"Trust God from the bottom of your heart; don't try to figure out everything on your own. Listen for God's voice in everything you do, everywhere you go; he's the one who will keep you on track."* Now the college tours had begun, decisions had to be made by May 1 and it was April 3. Everything started happening all at once and the decision on which college Kim would attend had to be decided quickly. How was college going to be paid for? Afterall, she graduated class salutatorian, and the buzz was it came with a monetary award. Her mother read the responses and one of them was a full 4-year ride because Kim graduated class salutatorian, I had to accept the offer soon. Thank you, Jesus, you right on time I DM-ed my friends that I was going to accept the offer of Morgan University and discovered two of us were going to Morgan U. As the time came close to school starting, Kim was nervous. She had not spent any time away from her family before, certainly not for lengthy periods of time, and was not sure where the money would come from for stuff she would need, but at least the education was paid for. Kim's grandma reminded her that she would never be alone that God is always with her Psalm 16:8 MSG *"Day and night I'll stick with GOD; I've got a good thing going and I'm not letting go."* Kim's mom had a college send off for her at her favorite restaurant and it was a fun and memorable time with family and friends.

After they got home, Kim's mom talked with her, and reminded her that she was designed for greatness, and it was time for her to walk into her future.

She reminded her about the sermon that was preached from "1 Samuel 17:40 *MSG* "*Then David took his shepherd's staff, selected five smooth stones from the brook, and put them in the pocket of his shepherd's pack, and with his sling in his hand approached Goliath.*" Don't forget God has gifted you with many talents, that you can use, when you need extra coins there's no need to be broke. You won't have to apply for a job, just focus on your inner abilities. Remember how you braided hair this summer and blinged out those Crocs? Girl, you got it in you!

<u>As Kim prepared for bed, she remembered the A.C.T.S.</u> *A(adoration), C(confession), T(thanksgiving) and S(supplication)* Christian prayer model and prayed to God.

""Father God, I honor and praise you for your goodness and confess that I have not always done what I should, but I am thankful for your grace and mercy toward me. I am asking that as I prepare to leave for college that you watch over my family. Keep my grandma, mom, and brothers in your care. Help me to stay focused and centered on my studies and who you called me to be. In Jesus name Amen".

The next few weeks went quickly, Kim was able to work at the local bakery/sandwich shop and save a little cash. As she began packing, Kim realized she would not see her grandma daily or hear her praying, but they certainly could face-time. Grandma promised her that they would face-time with each other daily to stay connected. "Of course, child," she said.

The next morning was moving day, Kim along with her mother and two brothers packed the car, for the drive to Morgan University. Kim could not believe this was happening! She had mixed emotions about leaving home but knew this was the only way to achieve her dreams.

Kim gave her grandma a hug and she whispered in her ear, "you'll do great things." Before letting go of each other, she slipped some money in Kim's pocket and said, "this is a little something to help with stuff." That was grandma, always making sure I had what was needed.

Kim enjoyed the Facetime calls from her grandma and looked forward to them. These calls helped her to stay connected to what was happening at home and gave her motivation.

The next few weeks were busy, finding classes, seeing friends, and getting adjusted. Finally meeting her roommate in person, they had met virtually over the summer and seemed to jell.

As Kim was preparing to leave for class, she received a call from her mother and could tell something was wrong. Her mom said grandma was in the hospital, but it was not anything to worry about, that grandma was just in for test. Kim wasn't sure but did not believe her and felt like she was hiding something. Kim even told her roommate there was more going on. She prayed that her grandma would get better. It became hard to concentrate on her studies, Kim needed to hear her grandma's voice. She called and she answered, sounding weak but still happy to hear from her, Kim certainly was. "grandma when are you going home?" She said "soon." After Kim talked with her grandma, she was more energized and ready to finish the semester and get home. The weeks could not go fast enough before it was time for winter break. She was excited, packed her gear the night before and was waiting for her mom to pick her up.

The ride home was quiet, and Kim sensed something was wrong. "How is grandma?" Her mom said "alright," that just did not feel right. When they arrived home, her mom told Kim she was in hospital again. I asked my mom "why didn't you tell me this on the way home?" My mother said, "I didn't want to upset you." Kim asked that she please take me to see her!! Kim arrived at the hospital, racing to her grandma's room. It really hurt Kim seeing her like that, she held her hand and prayed, she opened her eyes, "grandma it's me Kim, how are you feeling?" Grandma said, "Kim baby I'm fine how are you, child don't worry about me you just prayed no need to worry" 1 Peter 5:7 NLT *"Give all your worries and cares to God, for he cares about you."*

Kim stayed until visiting hours were over and then she kissed her grandma and left. She could not sleep worrying how her grandma was during the night. She heard her mom's phone ring and then heard her crying. She ran to her room and asked, "what was wrong?" "it's grandma she got her wings" I did not understand and said, "what do you mean?" Her mom says "she's gone" my heart sank! How could this be happening the woman who taught me to pray and have faith was gone. As the news of Kim's grandma's passing spread through the town, people came by their house, called, sent cards. It was overwhelming. There were more people than I realized my grandma had inspired, she was a celebrity.

My mom asked me to speak at my grandmother's funeral service and I did not know what to say. I could hear her voice saying, "pray about what to say." That was what she always did, prayed about everything before she did it. On the day of the service, I was overcome with emotion, but I prayed and felt better, now it was my turn to speak.

"My grandma was a woman of faith, she believed in God and the power of prayer.

Praying in the morning, during the day and night about everything.

My grandma taught me to pray and said, if you pray don't worry, she was dope no joke! Everyone showing up today is proof that she touched more people than I knew,

To me she was grandma, but she was also special to you.

If she were here today, she would say "all this for me?" I would tell her, "Why not girl you rock!"

Grandma thank you for teaching me to pray; thank you for believing in me, thank you for having confidence in me. Thank you for praying for us. Thank you for loving us.

Grandma, I love you.

After the service was over, the family hosted a reception. It was a beautiful gathering of grandma's family and friends. Talking with them at the reception gave me a feeling of comfort and let me know that my grandma shared her wisdom with everyone that she could.

When everyone left, the house had a strange quiet vibe. Kim's mom was sitting alone in the living room and called Kim and her siblings. "What's wrong?" She said, "now that Grandma is gone, we must keep her memory alive. My brother asked, "how do we do that?" Remember to pray, treat people with respect and show the love of God. John 15:12 NIV, *"My command is this: Love each other as I have loved you."*

The next few days were spent hanging out at home with my family, before returning to college. I even got to church! The time had come to return to college, and before leaving, Kim went into her grandma's room. Her chair was empty, but she could feel her spirit. She felt a certain closeness there. The time had come to return to college, and before leaving, Kim went into her grandma's room. Her chair was empty, but she could feel her spirit. Kim sat in her chair and started to pray. Her mom called out, "c'mon Kim it's time to go." She said, "ok mom." "Thank you, Grandma, for teaching me to pray!" Awright mom, I'm coming.

18

Printed in the United States
by Baker & Taylor Publisher Services